Ghost Face

GREG SANTOS

Ghost Face

Cover illustration by Alain Reno.
Author photograph by Mollye Miller.
Book designed and typeset by Primeau Barey, Montreal.
Edited by Jason Camlot.

Legal Deposit, Bibliothèque et Archives nationales du Québec
and Library and Archives Canada, 3rd trimester, 2020.

Library and Archives Canada Cataloguing in Publication
Title: Ghost face / Greg Santos.
Names: Santos, Greg, author.
Description: Poems.
Identifiers: Canadiana 20200189190 | ISBN 9781927599518 (softcover)
Classification: LCC PS8637.A584 G56 2020 | DDC C811/.6–DC23

For our publishing activities, DC Books gratefully acknowledges the financial support of SODEC and of the Government of Canada through Canadian Heritage and the Canada Book Fund. *Nous reconnaissons l'aide financière du gouvernement du Canada.*

Société de développement des entreprises culturelles Québec

Canada

Printed and bound in Canada.
Interior pages printed on Enviro Book, an environmentally responsible paper containing 100% post-consumer recycled fiber, processed chlorine-free and manufactured using biogas energy.
Distributed by Fitzhenry and Whiteside.

DC Books
5 Fenwick Ave.,
Montreal West, Quebec H4X 1P3
www.dcbooks.ca

for my parents

Contents

I.

I/YOU

There are many ghosts here. Listen, […]
– Bunkong Tuon

In the Memory Palace nothing is lost, just misplaced.
– James Tate

History

Thisishistory.Th
isishisstory.This
isherstory.Thisis
everyone'sstory.
Thisisnoone'sst
ory.Thisistheirst
ory.Thisismysto
ry.Thisisyoursto
ry.Thisisourstor
y.

Let's Start at the Beginning

You were adopted when you were a few months old. That you remember, right?

Now, who are you?

No. Pay attention.

Let me answer for you: You are nobody. You don't really exist.

That's not what I mean. You are a mask, a hoax, a scam, a con, a swindle. You are a ruse. You're pulling the wool over our eyes!

Hey now, I'm not the one on trial here.

I'm just trying to get to the bottom of things.

Siem Reap, Cambodia

Before stepping into a taxi
a young girl struggles to take the city with her:

Warm, sticky air bathing the street market,
comforting scent of fragrant rice,
pungent odor of dry fish,
raw flesh on butchers' hooks,
chickens squawking from wire pens,
crescendo of rickshaws, scooters, bicycles,
the city she will no longer call home.

As she speeds away, the city recedes into memory,
once dotted by women tending to the paddies,
the rolling countryside recedes into memory,
children splashing among water buffalo.

Now, echoes of distant missiles pierce her memories,
murders of crows dive into reddened fields.

The faces of Angkor watch
as their city crumbles,
as another one of their children flees,
taking nothing but me,
gently growing inside her.

Cambodian

Are you Cambodian?

So, were you born in Cambodia then?

Have you ever even been to Cambodia?

Then how can you consider yourself Cambodian?

How do you mean?

Most folks think you're Filipino. Remember when someone put you on a Twitter-thread for Filipino writers?

How did that make you feel?

It's the last name. Santos throws them off.

SANTOS. It's Portuguese, right?

Honestly, this is confusing…

It's like you are actually Cambodian or something…

Tiger Dream

His bellow echoes through the night.
Large head held upright,
dark eyes scanning the dense brush.
Ears dance, straining for the slightest sound.
The passing wind rustles the leaves,
releasing a cloud of blackened dust.
His nostrils dilate, snorting loudly at the breeze.
Moonlight cuts through the trees,
patterns the ornamented stone altar where he rests,
streaked fur undulating as his weight shifts.
In solitude he tenses his muscles,
arches his back and lifts his wide frame.
He circles himself,
paws padding the cool ground soundlessly.
Tufts of white fur under his mouth and eyes
contract as his face contorts into a grimace,
fangs exposed and vibrating
from a guttural growl directed at
something unnatural stirring in the dark.

Fu Manchu

When you grew out your moustache and goatee, did you get offended when they said you looked Asian?

...I didn't get offended.

You hesitated before answering. Not even just a little?

No.

C'mon, the Fu Manchu crack must've gotten you a little peeved.

... No.

Fine, suit yourself. By the way there's nothing wrong with being Asian. You said it yourself. It is part of your heritage.

I know that. But honestly, for a long time I
didn't even
consider myself Asian.
I didn't really know much about that side of my
background.

How did you remedy that?

Lots of searching. Books helped.

I'm Dog. Who Are You?

"People who thought differently were called worms, dogs, traitors."
– from an article in The New York Times *on the fallout of the Khmer Rouge and the Cambodian genocide*

I.
Once in a hospital waiting room with my father,
another child kept turning around to look at me,
singing *ching chong chow!*

His tinny song went on and on.
I did not know how to react.
Ignoring the boy did nothing.

My first response was to bare my teeth,
bark bark bark! I grinned, wild-eyed.
The boy hid. My father stared.

II.
When my children were younger they used to scream,
terrorized, running in the opposite
direction when a dog walked by.

In Cambodia, they once feared
Vach du Mach, One with the Gun,
coward who killed millions, his own people.

Words were used as knives.
Children would turn on their parents.
The wrong sentence was a life sentence.

III.
Pressing my whiskered face to theirs,
my children knead my fur
in their tiny hands.

I'm dog.
Embrace my dogness.
Are you dog, too?

Takeout

Remember when you went to grab Indian food for takeout and then you wanted to pick up cookies for yourself and M at that nice bakery near the apartment and you barged in holding that bag of vegetable biryani and malai kofta in that plastic bag and that old lady behind the counter looked really confused and yelled "Hey, did anyone order takeout? Nobody ordered takeout here. I'm sorry, nobody ordered takeout." And you said you just wanted to buy a cookie? LOL! There should be an emoji for biryani absurdism!

Juno

From an online description of the movie Juno (2007)

> *Juno is a whip-smart teen confronting an unplanned pregnancy by her classmate Bleeker. With the help of her best friend Leah, Juno finds her unborn child a "perfect" set of parents: an affluent suburban couple, Mark and Vanessa, longing to adopt. Luckily, Juno has the total support of her parents as she faces some tough decisions, flirts with adulthood and ultimately figures out where she belongs.*

Watching *Juno,* I couldn't help but see my birth mother as Juno. She must have been a whip-smart teen, too. She put me up for adoption when she was a young teen herself, probably just a couple years younger than Juno's character. And then there's Vanessa, the young wife who longs to have a baby of her own. She helped me gain a better appreciation of what my Mom must have experienced during the adoption process. But *Juno* was just a film and can't really show the ache in the chest of a young mother who watches her child being carried away, never to be seen again, or the elation of a woman who has just discovered over the phone that she is, after years of praying and waiting, a mother.

Murky Memories

after Charles Simic

Dad is running away breathlessly
on the treadmill.

Mom is confined in the attic
sorting the mess.

Dad is pounding
something in the tool room.

Mom is singing slightly off key
yet beautifully by the bed.

Dad is all alone
strumming his guitar on the porch.

Mom is choking back her own tears
as I bawl by the preschool window.

Dad is white
from his shaving cream.

Mom is perched high atop a chair
removing a dead light bulb.

Dad and Mom bow their heads in silence
as I murmur last rites upon my hamster.

Childhood

Taking Polaroid pictures of my Transformers.

Dancing to Michael Jackson's "Smooth Criminal" before my parents' mirror.

Pretending the pool-cleaning robot was a sea monster.

Wrestling with Tata, my grandmother, breaking her glasses.

Making my pet rock its cloth bed, tightening its leash.

My goldfish, Tom, Jerry.

My hermit crabs, Big Bertha, Hermie.

My dwarf hamsters, Nutmeg, Tiger, Lucky.

My Sea Monkeys: Sharky, Fin, Minnie, Mickey, George,
Tiny Tim, Moe, Cutie Pie, Cuddles, Flip, Sprinkle,
Joy, Micro Machine, Bumblebee, Marco, Polo,
Chocolate Chip…

At the barber hiding *Playboy* in *The Economist.*

My terror of clowns.

My parents paying my birthday clown to leave.

Book gift from my parents: *Why Was I Adopted?*

My longstanding belief in ghosts.

Zazen

a haibun

He decorated his bedroom with bamboo wallpaper. It's still like that now. He adores noodles and is good with chopsticks. As a teenager, he was obsessed with Zen Buddhism, accosting friends with koans he thought he understood. When he greets people, he tends to give a slight bow. He earned a blue belt in karate and took Tai Chi lessons. He took a Bushido class – lasted four weeks. He kept lucky bamboo on a shelf, greeting the sun by his bedroom window. He owned numerous t-shirts from Urban Outfitters with what was possibly Japanese text printed on them.

Dear lucky bamboo
bowing to the sun. What is
your original face?

Khmer for Baby

In my

past life

did I have a name

or was I

just *tearok*?

Journal Entry

"If I ever visit Cambodia,
I wonder what it will be like
to be met with smiling faces
that look like mine?
Will I feel at home
or utterly alone?"

I asked this question
before I had my children.

My links
to my past
present
and future.

Nicknames

My parents called each other *chuchi.*
Was it short for those 80s Monchhichi dolls?

I don't really know what a *chocolatito plus* is
but it was my father's term of endearment for me.

My family referred to me as *el niño.*
Both a dear one and an extreme climate event.

Our Name

Can I ask you something?

Yes.

What was your name?

I don't know.

What do you mean you don't know?

I don't know if you don't know.

But we have a blood connection.

Yes.

Do you know if we had any siblings?

… A sister named Preah Neang.

Whoa. Really? Do you know what that name means?

It means princess in Khmer.

That's amazing. How did you know that?

I Googled it. Or how about Pich. That means diamond.

Oh.

An Open Book

a haibun

Was he an artist? An armchair philosopher? Did he wear glasses, too? Work as a mechanic? Did his laugh sound like mine? Was he of royal birth? A long-lost prince, perhaps? Reclusive Zen monk. One who fell in love with a young girl and strayed from his calling. A street musician who played a weathered violin. Royal family portrait painter. Was he an awkward teenager? Or a confident valedictorian? Was he naturally athletic and good at soccer? Did he hunt or fish? Was he a young soldier who dreamed of studying at The Sorbonne? Did he cautiously hide Western classics under a cellar door?

The boy takes out an
origami library book.
Dreams of paper cranes.

Question

Why are you writing this?

We were both born without memories.

I am writing our memories for us.

Absence

We exist
in a world
of slashes.

Bound
not by blood,
but by absence.

Our fathers
are
ghosts.

Amnesiac

It all happened a long time ago.
Do you remember?
I think there was a nun, a war,
the phone call that changed everyone's lives.
No, how could you remember? You weren't even there.
But now that I think about it, neither was I.

That moment when you have something to say but
forget what you've been saying mid-sentence,
I have that right now.
I've had that problem my entire life.

My history is made of tweezers
removing a splinter from a child's palm,
afternoon swims in the plastic turtle pool out back,
white bread salami sandwiches.
Thank goodness history isn't all goblets and tapestries.

Reaching a clearing in the woods,
I take a moment to consider my travels.
The villagers were right:
the view is, indeed, magnificent.

Forgetfulness

I don't want to forget.

Sometimes it's necessary to forget.

Forgetfulness dulls the sharp edges that cut too deep.

I need to remember so that they are not lost.

This is a present for my children to one day remember.

You Remember

after Joe Brainard

You remember how he always said elephants never forget.

You remember watching reruns of Get Smart on YTV and thinking how much they looked like Maxwell Smart and Agent 99 from pictures when they were younger.

You remember him bouncing a soccer ball on his head, knees, feet, like a Hacky Sack.

You remember seeing him cry three times in your life: When Littlefoot's mother died in *The Land Before Time.* When Bambi's mother died. That morning in the kitchen soon after you all learned he had cancer. He held your hand and told you he was scared.

You remember watching him shave. You sat in the hallway chair that faced the bathroom. He was wearing a white undershirt, matching boxer shorts, and a white Santa Claus beard.

You remember playing ping pong with him one summer vacation. You don't remember who won or where it was.

You remember going out for lunch with a friend and being late coming back for math class. You were running through the school, when a teacher saw you and told you to go to the office right away.

You remember thinking you were in big trouble but then you spotted your mother's colleague from the office who told you there had been some complications.

You remember nervously asking him for advice about girls. You don't remember what he said specifically but you do remember that it suddenly made the mystery of girls make sense.

You remember your grandmother wailing, "The doctors killed him, the doctors killed him…"

You remember wanting to say goodbye, to say more than you had that last morning.

You remember doing French homework with him in the kitchen. You have a photograph of the two of you sitting side by side, reading intently.

You remember reading *Calvin and Hobbes* on the carpet in the living room while he browsed through *The Montreal Gazette.*

You remember his band playing covers of The Beatles, Roch Voisine, The Gypsy Kings, Elvis… in the basement while you lip-synched and acted out the lyrics with friends in the driveway.

You remember–despite the glaring lights of the theatre–that you were still able to spot their bright faces in the audience. You were dressed-up as a disheveled hobo on stage.

You remember stepping into the audience to ask for spare change and how he dropped a dollar (or was it a quarter?) into your hat. That was the first time you were paid to use your imagination.

You remember listening to him on the answering machine tape over and over afterwards to be certain you didn't forget what his voice sounded like.

You remember his cooking skills were limited to sunny-side-up eggs, made with the magical combination of equal parts olive oil and butter.

You remember the morning he was supposed to start his treatment. You told him not to worry, that everything would be fine, and that you loved him.

You remember he said, "What a son, what a son…"

You remember the silent drive to the hospital and the long walk through the hallways that echoed and seemed stretched out like a gothic cathedral.

You remember being led into the room and being told by a disembodied voice (you don't remember whose) that he was gone. An allergic reaction to his treatment.

You remember having dreams about him afterwards. He would step out of the fog, casually ask you how things were going. Then he'd fill you in on what heaven was like.

You never remembered what he said.

You remember wishing that he could visit your mother in her dreams, too.

You remember that odd relief you felt when you learned about his cancer. More terrifying was the void of not knowing.

You remember being alone in the theatre not long after he died. You were going over your lines when you heard his voice call out your name. You searched frantically backstage, behind every curtain, in every dark corner.

You remember his drawing skills being limited to elephants. Yet you still wish you were able to draw them as well as he did.

You remember how he always said elephants never forget.

You remember wishing you could transform yourself into an elephant.

II.

SAUDADE

Saudade is a Portuguese expression that is almost untranslatable. The best way to describe it is: the presence of absence. It is a longing for someone or something that you remember fondly but know you can never experience again.

– Laurie Burrows Grad,
"Saudade: The Presence of Absence",
Huffington Post

I don't always remember
where I come from

in my sleep,
my dreams remind me
who I am

never will my roots
leave me.

– Joséphine Bacon

Dear Ghosts

One cold rainy spring evening
as I was drifting off to sleep
M showed me a passage
from a new book.

> *Here, a part about the universe:*
> *Atoms.*

Atoms, such a beautiful word.
Like cellar door and hope.

> *Read this.*
> *You might want it for your book.*

In it, I read how when things die,
their atoms don't disappear or cease to exist
but are redistributed.

An ancient fern becomes coal.
This lump of coal begets a diamond.
And on and on until
the atoms of the fern are nothing but

a speck

in the web of my open palm.

Your faces flash
in the attic of my memory.
You are welcome spirits.

I toss off the covers, rush to my office.
I am struggling to capture this moment,
how do I grasp onto these silvery apparitions?

The moment is gone
and I'm left gasping
grasping for something to hold.

The distant sound of our dishwasher,
some light rain outside, and it's
gone gone gone.

Redistributed away.

Dear ghosts,
where do your atoms reside?

Father.

Tata. Nano. Vovo. Chico. My grandparents.

The birth family I never knew.

I like to think that you still inhabit our planet.

We contain multitudes, right?

The galaxy in the speck of a birthmark–
the one that I call my chocolate spot
my *chocolatito plus*
that cannot be smudged off.

A planet. A galaxy.
The cosmos. Heaven.

In the palm of my hand.
The size of a mustard seed.
Head of a needle.
Where angels reside.

Humberto Santos, 1967

After a hard day's night at Sir George Williams night school
he puts his commerce textbooks away,
calls his parents to wish them goodnight.

"*Boa noite, mãe,*"
he whispers to his mother.
"*Boa noite, Humberto,*" she replies.

He's worked hard this week,
but Friday's here, it's time to play hard.
He reaches under his bed, pulls out a sleek guitar case.

He flicks the clasps open: *clip, clap, clithk*
"It's been a hard day's night,
and I been working like a dog…"

Tomorrow he plans to see the Great Britain pavilion
to browse for new Beatles records,
maybe even visit Greece.

Who knows? Perhaps, he'll go to La Ronde,
bump into the likes of Prince Rainier and Grace Kelly.
He is after all, in the cosmopolitan city of Montreal.

He cradles his beloved Goya classical guitar,
plucks the strings with his fingers,
begins playing a bouncy tune

"Olha que coisa mais linda, mais cheia de graça…"
His head bouncing in the moonlight,
he quietly sings to himself:

"Tall and tan and young and lovely,
the girl from Ipanema goes walking..."
Closing his eyes, he's whisked to the beaches of Cascais.

He's in his hometown walking barefoot on the coastline,
smells sardines being grilled,
and kettles cooking chips.

"Oh, but I watch her so sadly,
how can I tell her I love her?"

Within the Memory Palace

after James Tate

You remember taking your first bite of caribou,
hanging from the side of a reservoir,
somehow losing your glasses and shoes in the same night,
being deathly afraid of helicopters,
running, running for your life and never looking back.
You had a happy childhood.
Then you awoke in a strange town,
you were at a party, off in some corner alone.
Someone kissed you in the dark.
You stopped running and learned to appreciate
strolls through marshes and sand dunes.
You even had a chance to sit on a wicker chair for a spell.
But the running of your youth was replaced by train tracks,
watching the horizon rise and fall while at sea,
flying over cliffs and dazzling cities.
An exquisite afternoon tea service,
getting caught in a rainstorm in church,
a honeymoon in Rhode Island,
push push push, you're doing great!

Invisible Guests

New Haven, Connecticut

Alone in our apartment
I notice how quiet it really is without you.

The creak of my chair, the clicks as I type,
my breathing, the hum of the fridge:

sounds I took for granted,
amplified by your absence.

Tapping from within the walls, mice perhaps,
dull breathing of heating vents, the apartment

filling with invisible guests.
I put on Louis Armstrong and Ella Fitzgerald.

Phantom voices
to keep me company.

Under My Bed

I keep my umbilical cord in a box.
Nobody knows of its existence but me.

Every night I take it out of its snug home,
recite prayers to it before sleeping.

I'm not sad but I cannot stop crying.
It sings lullabies to soothe my colicky brain.

It twitches at the sound of my voice,
sometimes curves into a crimson grin.

That Moment

My mind is doing jumping jacks.
Only my beloved, our doctor, and I know.

I am used to sending off my poems into the unknown.
They go forth like little pioneers.

But this is different.
It is the hum before the computer shuts down.

It is that moment after the movie trailers end
but before the feature presentation begins.

The exact second when the dog
spots the popcorn on its way to the floor.

It is the tick before the tock,
the instant before the clock strikes midnight.

That jolt of electricity before lips first touch.
It is the moment before the line turned blue.

And again the moment before another turned blue
a second time, just to be sure.

First Cold

My newborn son balls up his fists,
diminutive pugilist.

A first cold is a badge
on the sash of life, I suppose.

It doesn't make his suffering any easier.
A damp face cloth is small comfort.

A pain that pulses deep in my chest–
ache that suddenly drops into my gut,

an elevator plummeting down an endless shaft–
I can't get the image right!

That feeling of helplessness,
guilt for not being able to take away our children's hurt,

to swipe it into oblivion
like an icon from a screen.

Tiny Wolves

It's three in the morning.
Our child's puny whimpers echo throughout the night.

The tiny wolves living in the depths of our cupboards
respond with their own knowing howls.

They watch over us in the darkness.
I'm grateful for their nightlight eyes.

Fog-Mind

You enter
a wilderness.
Another flare-up.

Bats in an attic,
your thoughts get locked in together,
wings jostling.

You feel your heart racing,
you put your fingers to your neck,
your wrist, back to your chest.

No sign of a heartbeat.
Did it somehow sneak out of your chest,
a thief into the night?

You focus on the crack of moonlight
through the door.
Maybe your heart snuck out that way.

You somehow remember the moon is a mirror.
That thought momentarily comforting,
before you cloud over once again.

You can only wait
for this fog-mind to dissipate.
How long will it last?

Three Amigos

for J and R

The three of us
bundled at night in winter coats.

Lugging fireworks from Brockville,
cheap matches, wine.

My first visit back since moving,
we wanted the fireworks to make up for lost time.

Passing the bottle between us,
among skeletal jungle gyms, creak of metal swings.

We grasp the flimsy matches with cold claw hands,
striking them, followed swiftly by a phosphorus hiss.

The lit fuse sends us running in opposite directions
to witness, apart, a burst of light, a flash of confetti.

The Memory Game

a cento after John Ashbery

For a while we caught the spirit of things
as they had drifted in the past.
Was it for this we eschewed attention-getting moments
in the plaza after the sun finished sulking?

It all happened long ago –
Today it's clear the rent has come due again.
It's only a shred, really, a fragment of life.
It will be over in a minute, you said.
Still at it, friend?

Amorous ghosts will pursue us for a time,
once that happens you can forget the context
you will leave empty-handed.

Who knew it would be this silly, and so dense?
Prop up "the meaning,"
let there be some refreshing
gents, off on a new tangent.

O I tell you,
It's quite simple, really:
Wait – suddenly I can't think of any!
And he was lost, gibbering on the coast of
bright nights, lit sea, buttered roofs, dandelion breath.

Pleasant memories are just that.
Would you say those figures are accurate?
Why not? I'm game.

Elegy for September 19th

In Quebec, September 19th was named the official Memorial Day dedicated to all the missing, dead, and the ancestors of the Cambodian people affected by genocide perpetuated by the Khmer Rouge regime from 1975-1979.

My wife had gotten me *First They Killed My Father* by Cambodian author Loung Ung for my birthday. The book was such a visceral and heart-wrenching experience. Ung spoke from a child's point of view of the carnage that befell Cambodia. I couldn't help but project that onto what my birth mother and my ancestors went through. Her story was our story. Then I watched the Angelina Jolie-directed Netflix film inspired by the book and I just needed to exorcise what was swirling in my head.

I visited Montreal's Wat Buddha Sodhara Temple Bouddhique in 2017. It was my first visit to a Buddhist temple. I wanted to pay respects to my ancestors, but I went alone and I was intimidated. When I first arrived, a monk in an orange robe with a stern look opened the door. I said I was there for the ceremony and I stammered that I was, um, Cambodian, it's ah, it's a long story… He sized me up, grunted, turned around, walked away. Was this a big mistake?

Thankfully another gentleman, slim with a head full of dark curly waves like my son, greeted me, and I told him my story. I soon met others who helped me feel welcomed. I sat cross-legged on woven red and yellow mats with them and prayed, listened to Khmer, not understanding anything but the words happily ping-ponged around my skull. We paid tribute to the monks at a shrine for the dead and missing.

Then there was the feast. Bowl after bowl after bowl was brought out: rice, noodles, vibrant yellow, green, and red curries, watermelon, grapes, other fruits, pickles vegetables, pork, beef, and other meats galore. First the monks ate and then the food was offered to our ancestors, before we dug in.

Death is a Man Who Feels Scared

Bains Corner, New Brunswick

Trudging over fickle ice crystals,
moss brittle, trees broken,

collecting slight sheets
of birch bark for scribbling,

we hear something cry out
deep in the brush.

What was it?
A deer, perhaps.

A song of sadness,
anger, hunger.

I am compelled to sing back
but what could I possibly say?

Pebbles

"The attacks themselves are minimal in their destructive power, like pebbles thrown in a pond; it is the shock waves they set off which are the real danger."
– from Non-state Threats and Future Wars,
edited by Robert J. Bunker, 2002

Here you
come, dear
forsaken ones,
the forever
stained.

Never to reveal
your tortured
consciences.
Would your
words even matter?

Nestled among
loved ones,
we take
our chances
living, making
earth fertile,

while waters
will always
toss pebbles
like you
against sand.

We will
walk freely
across streets
like wind
through plains.

In cities,
we will toil,
continue to laugh,
love. Despite you,
our willful
hearts pulse.

My Grandmother's Recipe

I.
I have yet to dust off my Tata's recipe for *croquettas de atún.*
I still have not gotten the hang of béchamel, the mother of all sauces.
My daughter does not eat fish, also a factor.

Learning to cook tuna fritters just how my grandmother used to
is on my perpetual to-do list, like getting my driver's license.
It has been one year today since she died.

II.
My Mother once told me she couldn't stand how people say
passed away, such a feeble euphemism.
The words numbing in their uncertainty.

Her side of the family in Spain lived through *La Guerra,* its aftermath.
With both my maternal grandparents now dead,
I have no access to their memories but from second-hand stories.

III.
Throughout my childhood, in works of literature, art, Picasso's *Guernica,*
Pan's Labyrinth, my love of Lorca, a perpetual feeling of *duende.*
I've come to glean fragments, which I'm only now piecing together.

My Spanish grandmother and Italian
grandfather's revulsion
upon naming any of *Los Tres Dictatores*:
Franco, Mussolini, Castro.

Showing off a photo of my newborn daughter raising one
tiny fist up in the air
someone remarked we have a *communista* in the making,
the joke was met with a frown and a prayer. *We do not joke
about such things.*

IV.
I learned that my Mother and Tia were sent off
to live with relatives when they were children during the
Franco years.
This fact was always kept in the fog of the past.

Tata worked as a waitress at her family's restaurant by
the beach.
Nano, my grandfather, stationed nearby as a soldier.
Noticing my grandmother,
he asked her out on a date for ice cream. A sweet story
amidst darkness.

V.
Once when I told her of my calling to be a writer, she
didn't flinch.
She was in awe of the magic of Hollywood stars like Doris
Day, Clark Gable.
She told me of her enduring dream to write stories and
movie scripts.

But she was told that it would never happen to her.
Writing stories for movies was unladylike, she would wistfully say.
It was a different world, a different time. *Que sera, sera…*

VI.
I will one day learn to cook her *croquettas de atún.*
Until then, I write this for her,
my recipe keeping Tata's story alive. *Whatever will be, will be…*

Rainbow Fish

a haibun

Dad showed up in my dream again. It has been a while. Waking up foggy this morning, I was gasping to make some sense of it all. I barely remembered, then suddenly it came, a rainbow fish swimming into view through the murk. I was in his office at my childhood home, he had a present for us! It was a box, transparent, and fringed with gold. Inside was a delicate chain necklace with a clear pyramid hanging from its end. The pyramid glittered, a prism in the sunlight. Inside it were tiny flowers, flowers of lace like baby's breath, but sweet smelling. Cinnamon, I think lavender, several other spices I can't remember. Dad's voice said it was for us. I looked around. I don't know where his voice was coming from. He was no longer in the room. The kids were beaming with excitement. I told them, be careful. Be careful with Grandpapa's glass box. But I was smiling, too. Before the dream mottled away into wakefulness.

This tremendous fish
under marble rainbow skies
half out of water.

III.

ODE TO JOY

Only on varied diet can we live.
The pious fable and the dirty story
Share in the total literary glory.
–W. H. Auden

O the joy of my spirit! It is uncaged!
It darts like lightning!
–Walt Whitman

Work Smoothly, Lifetime Peace

Listening to a recording of Allen Ginsberg reading "Angkor Wat"

Looking up
at our skyscrapers of elephantine bigness
I was walking in downtown Montreal
on Ste Catherine Street
feeling tiny
heading home after going to a dentist appointment
just a routine checkup & a cleaning
no cavities
my kids would be proud of me
I am snaking through
forever construction pilons
suddenly
I am set upon by a Buddhist monk
his head shaved
of undeterminable age
could be mid-50s to 70s I guess
I bow in politeness
he smiles
eyes crinkled crows feet
he points to a sheet of paper

PEACE = $20

I'm bewildered
running on autopilot
tells me to sign my name
I do: GREG
I sign to donate $20 dollars for peace
one heck of a bargain

for a lifetime of peace
I feel heavy
like a stone statue
feet planted to the concrete
in a swift serpentine movement
& with a quick smile
the monk slips on a dark
red cranberry-coloured
wooden bead bracelet
smooth around my left wrist
he hands me a golden ticket
goes on his merry monk way
I turn the amulet in my hand.
on one side an etching of
Namas Guanyin Bodhisattva
sitting on a lotus blossom
one hand raised up
underneath in rainbow Chinese lettering:

Kai guang Amu let

I flip the golden ticket amulet over:

WORK
SMOOTHLY

LIFETIME
PEACE

I get home and look it up.
Is this a legitimate Buddhist practice?
It's got to be some kind of a scam
I find a *New York Times* article about it
I could have said no
just walked away
but what if
what if it's not...

I show it to my wife & kids
they're polite but wary

wait how much did you give?

I display the amulet & bracelet
on my writing desk

jot down in my bullet planner

daily goal: work smoothly
longterm goal: lifetime peace

scam or not
I'll take this surprise
pep talk
from my ancestors

Montreal, June 12, 2019

Shall We Dance?

The Mars InSight Lander
touched down on the red planet
on November 26, 2018.
I am 37 years old.
At the beginning of December,
some space wind blows past a seisometer
and is recorded by NASA to study Marsquakes.
How odd it feels to write down that word!
On this date, December 7 2018,
as my children cut through water
during their swimming lessons,
twirling about as if in zero gravity,
I click on a link from my laptop.
Wind blasts across the Lander's solar panels
and I am an earthling on this tiny blue planet
listening to Martian wind for the first time.
Today I get a haircut,
shrug on a blazer for an evening party,
mingle amid the clinking of wine glasses.
We celebrate the holidays.
Listen.
Heard best with headphones,
can you hear that low pitch?
It is Mars's heartbeat.
There is so much darkness right now,
the building of walls,
our deep-rooted fear of aliens.
Yet we are alive.
We are alive to hear a Martian zephyr,

so privileged to hear the first sounds
ever recorded on another planet.
Today I woke up to my son snuggling me,
awakened by his words,
"You are the best daddy ever."
I feel so lucky.
To be the best daddy ever.
To be alive right now.
I admit I do not always feel this grateful.
Small irritants, micro-aggressions
have a tendency to ruin the day.
The gravity of our world
always pushing down on our fragile bodies.
We are not always thankful.
But today I am.
I hope you are, too.
For an instant in the grand scheme of things,
I am thankful.
To feel this alien wind blow across my heart
is but a reminder that I have lived
to hear my children's breath,
a zephyr,
a reminder that I am sharing this tender moment
between our planet and Mars.

Dear Earthlings and Martians,
may we continue sharing this
grateful space dance together for eons.

Ode to Joy

There's something in the way you say papoose.
A nail file can come in handy in a jail cell in Mexico,
Universal City, CA.

Row boats are especially romantic during foggy weather.
Has anyone in chaps ever said you look fetching in
peacock feathers?

For the record, crazy glue much prefers to be called
"usefully eccentric" glue.
Don't worry, the scream coming from behind the closed
door is from a spirit tickle-fight.

Might I interest you in some cocktail nuts, friend?
No need to get fidgety, our flight is scheduled to last for
only just a few more time zones.

Crystal Pepsi

I watch you asleep in your crib.
My heart, a pulsar emitting beams of light.

Like hummingbirds your eyelids flicker,
here I am wishing I were a net.

When I am away from you
my heart calls out a plaintive whale song.

I must admit, I find this startling
when I am showering or on the web.

They say you cannot hold onto a snowflake,
but if Pepsi can create clear cola, what, then, is
not possible?

Scary Stories to Tell in the Dark

Do not enter gingerbread houses,
no matter how enticing the icing.
Do not take candy from
the children of strangers.
Saying Bloody Mary three times
facing a mirror in the dark is a no no.
Whatever you do, don't leave your foot
dangling over the bed overnight.
Skulking through the woods
and the wind whispers your name,
oh boy, that's the Wendigo, my child.
In Cambodia, they are taught to fear the Ahp,
also known as Krasue in Thailand.
These apparitions are usually women,
their faces, young and beautiful.
If you are to look down, they are bodyless.
The Ahp is but a floating head,
their spine, guts, icky entrails,
are all that's left dangling in mid-air.
See their hovering glow and you're a goner.
The Khmer people keep a spirit house near their homes.
These stilted wooden structures
lead ghosts like Ahps away from the living.
Burn some fake money
to keep them feeling wealthy.
Leave a snack for them to nosh on,
sticky rice, fruits, coconuts,
donuts are a good bet
since ghosts have sweet tooths, duh.
Sport a red bracelet or tie a red string

around your wrist,
doing so will keep your soul
from being whisked away from your body.
The string reminds you to
practice compassion and kindness.
Red is the colour of good luck and bravery.
They say red makes people hungry, too.
It's also my son's favourite colour,
so there's that.
You know what they say,
happy ghosts don't bother the living.
Therefore, keep a whoopie cushion,
joy-buzzer, and a joke book
on your person at all times.
Cross your fingers, knock on wood,
super glue a penny to your hand.
Heck, toss your old wardrobe out the window,
wear red from head to toe, just to be safe.
See, Good Luck will follow you,
skipping down the sidewalk,
her braids bobbing with every leap,
to the ends of time,
maybe even longer.

Action!

I hopped onto the Metro.
The water pickpocketed his swimming trunks.

Her boots reflected the northern lights.
My spear leaned against the ancient tree and had a catnap
under the shade.

The accordion is on its last wheeze.
The vending machine isn't really out of change; it's
just greedy.

The subway pole likes to be held by strangers.
My fingernails tease my toenails about their looks.

The leather backpack dreams of grazing in a pasture by a
red barn
but forgets its dreams in the morning.

The salt and pepper shaker gossip about the bread basket.
Short espresso is addicted to heartache.

Dear Dad,

The children
are asleep, you
watch me from
photo frames.

It is raining on Good Friday.
An April shower,
intermittent taps and
drips on the office window.

It is nice to feel
the warmth of your smile
again, even if they're just
pictures.

April is your birthday month.

Our crocuses have not yet
peeked out of the ground.
Out of the dead land.
Still we wait.
Our children remain excited to discover snowdrops.

Our two children.
Your grandchildren – wolfed down
tartes au sucre at a sugar shack
near Mont-Saint-Grégoire this past week.
I'm sure your infamous sweet tooth –
the one your granddaughter inherited –
would heartily approve.

Watching Mary Magdalene (2019)
Tonight, On Demand, I wonder

what you would have thought of the movie.
Joaquin Phoenix looking much older than
the 33 years Jesus would have been.
I guess, it makes some sense.
Jesus would have had several
gray hairs by then, worry lines,
bags under his eyes.

    Are you surprised I'm nearly 40?
    I've been alive longer than the amount of years
        I knew you...

The sweeping panoramas of Magdala and Galilee
would have impressed you.
They remind me of the ocean and cliffs near Cascais.

We went there years ago when we only had one
    infant child:

    I recall *pasteis de belem, pasteis de bacalhau,*
    getting pickpocketed on the tram in Lisboa,
    eating *pata negra jamon,*
    the sand between our daughter's toes making her squeal,
    later whisking her to the hospital due to fever and
        a bad cough,
    being grateful for her Portuguese card,
    thanks to you.

This Lenten season is a time of reflection,
of loss, of contemplation –

        your face often appears to me when I am idle.

                                It is a welcome distraction.

A respite from anxiety,
the fog and fatigue that creeps up on me
when I want it least.

My amygdala warning me of
invisible, imaginary threats,
I cannot tell if they are real or not.

Do you know that we've seen
images of a black hole?
Scientists from around the world
made an earth-sized telescope.

The image of a black hole,
the light around the gaping darkness
looks like your wedding band,
it swirls in my imagination.

Notre-Dame de Paris nearly burnt down, too,
and scientists were able to partially revive
pigs' brains four hours after death.
What did those pigs dream
when their minds were briefly reanimated?

Oh, to go back over 20 years and to have you back
just long enough to say goodbye!

That missing goodbye is something I frequently regret.
I was out at a food court with A,
one of the few times during the week that we
were allowed to dine outside of school grounds.
I tell myself, I should have been at school.

We live lives of so many shoulds.

Maybe then they would have warned me in time…

I know.

I know, it's useless to want to change the past–
that doesn't make me want to change the outcome any
less urgently.

I haven't written much lately,
so this sudden jostling
is an unexpected gift.
Thank you.

It makes me want to hurry, as if I don't have much time left
to be awake.

We are always one step closer to death.

I think of Mark Strand and how he wrote how Death was
waiting for him,
leaning back in his chair and stroking his beard:

I am not thinking of Death, but Death is thinking of me.

What is Death like?

Are you waiting for me,
a blanket of stars spread across your thighs?

A glass paperweight on my desk,
an amber sphere, flecked with gold
flakes suspended and draped as if

a tablecloth for one of Mom's epic
Easter lamb family dinners.
Green, blue flecks swirling around
this tiny galaxy in my hand.

Is heaven like this?
So ornate, so eerily perfect?

On your birthday at the start of April,
I found that cassette tape you used to record
The Santos Band in 1990, a recording of you
rehearsing for the show with your buddies.
The other side of the cassette, the big night:
performing A Hard Day's Night, La Bamba,
Chuck Berry's Johnny Be Good…

Listening to the tape,
I am grateful to hear the strums,
rhythms of your voice again.
Another gift.

It is time for me to get some sleep.

Let's do this again sometime.

Montreal, April 19, 2019

Notes

My gratitude to the editors of the following publications for publishing earlier versions of the poems found in *Ghost Face:*

Matter: A Journal of Poetry and Political Commentary, Cha: An Asian Literary Journal, World Literature Today, Ricepaper, Montréal Writes, Montreal Serai, Vallum, Matrix, and *Voicemail Poems.*

"Pebbles" was featured in *Our Willful Hearts: Selections from Re-Creating Home.* The proceeds for this anthology and its accompanying gala were done in support of a refugee family making a new life in Quebec.

The following poems also appear in the poetry pamphlet, *Blackbirds* (Eyewear, 2018): "Siem Reap, Cambodia" and "I'm Dog. Who Are You?"

"Amnesiac" also appears in my debut full-length poetry book, *The Emperor's Sofa* (DC Books, 2010).

"Work Smoothly, Lifetime Peace" was written while listening to a recording of Allen Ginsberg reading his long poem "Angkor Wat" from the SpokenWeb Montreal website. Ginsberg's reading was originally recorded at Sir George Williams University, Montreal, 1969. It can be heard at the following link: https://montreal.spokenweb.ca/sgw-poetry-readings/allen-ginsberg-at-sgwu-1969/

Being the Canadian-born son of Cambodian refugees and the adopted son of European immigrants, I have long grappled with questions of my identities. Writing this book has helped me unpack and embrace my families' multi-layered histories.

For further reading about Cambodian, refugee, and transracial adoptee literature, I would recommend the following works:

Gruel, Bunkong Tuon

And So I Was Blessed, Bunkong Tuon

First They Killed My Father: A Daughter of Cambodia Remembers, Loung Ung

Inside Out & Back Again, Thanhha Lai

Older Sister. Not Necessarily Related., Jenny Heijun Wills

The Doctor Will Fix It, Bunkong Tuon

A Nail the Evening Hangs On, Monica Sok

Acknowledgements

Besos and blessings to my parents and family. Pursuing this writing dream of mine, with your love and encouragement, has meant the world to me. My hope is that I honour our families' stories with this book.

The section tilted 'I/You' was started during my time as a graduate student at The New School (2007-2009). I am grateful to Honor Moore for her guidance in her memoir writing class.

Thank you to Joshua Levy, Ryan Schachter, Bunkong Tuon, Gabino Iglesias, Gillian Sze, Tammy Ho Lai-Ming, Klara du Plessis, Cora Siré, Marcela Huerta, Larissa Andrusyshyn, Zsolt Alapi, Ben Tanzer, Zoe Shaw, and Jenny Heijun Wills. I am honoured to call you my friends. I am grateful to you all for inspiring me to keep growing as a person and a writer.

This book would not have been possible without the enthusiastic support of my editor, Jason Camlot, and Keith Henderson, my publisher at DC Books.

To my wife, Maryn, thank you for talking literature and the mysteries of the universe with me and for coming up with the book's title. To my dear children, Rosemary and Arthur, thank you for keeping me young at heart. You three are my muses forever.

Greg Santos is the author of *Blackbirds* (2018), *Rabbit Punch!* (2014), and *The Emperor's Sofa* (2010). He holds an MFA in Creative Writing from The New School. He regularly works with at-risk communities as a creative writing instructor and he teaches at the Thomas More Institute. He is the Editor in Chief of the Quebec Writers' Federation's online literary journal, *carte blanche.* He is an adoptee of Cambodian, Spanish, and Portuguese descent. He lives in Tiohtià:ke/Montréal with his wife and two children. *Ghost Face* is his third full-length poetry collection with DC Books. Author's website: gregsantos.me